WE CAN READ

Senior Authors
Carl B. Smith
Virginia A. Arnold

Linguistics Consultant
Ronald Wardhaugh

Macmillan Publishing Co., Inc.
New York
Collier Macmillan Publishers
London

Copyright © 1983 Macmillan Publishing Co., Inc.

All rights reserved. No part of this book may be reproduced or transmitted in any form or by any means, electronic or mechanical, including photocopying, recording, or by any information storage and retrieval system, without permission in writing from the Publisher.

ACKNOWLEDGMENTS

The publisher gratefully acknowledges permission to reprint the following copyrighted material:

"City," by Langston Hughes. Copyright © 1958 by Langston Hughes. Reprinted by permission of Harold Ober Associates Incorporated.

"How to Tell the Top of a Hill" from *The Reason for the Pelican* by John Ciardi. Copyright © 1959 by John Ciardi. By permission of J. B. Lippincott, Publishers.

Illustrations: Ray Cruz, pp. 2-3; Carolyn McHenry, pp. 4-11; Nancy Munger, pp. 12-19; David Chestnutt, pp. 20-21; Len Ebert, pp. 22-29; Olivia Cole, pp. 30-31; Bruce Lemerse, pp. 32-39; Angela Adams, pp. 42-51; Jan Pyk, pp. 52-61; Olivia Cole, pp. 62-63. **Photographs:** Norman Prince, pp. 32-37; Tommy Wadelton/Shostal Associates, Inc., p. 38; Farrell Grehan/Photo Researchers, Inc., p. 39; Colour Library International, pp. 40-41.
Cover Design: Jan Pyk

Macmillan Publishing Co., Inc.
866 Third Avenue, New York, New York 10022
Collier Macmillan Canada, Inc.

Printed in the United States of America
ISBN 0-02-131680-5
9 8 7 6 5 4 3

Contents

Ben the Bird,
 a mystery by Peter Martin Wortmann 4

Ted Paints, *a story* 12

How to Tell the Top of a Hill,
 a poem by John Ciardi 20

Little Red, *a story by Judith Davis* 22

SKILLS: **Beginning Sounds** .. 30

In the Country,
 a photo-essay by Judith Davis 32

City, *a poem by Langston Hughes* 40

The Party, *a story by Judith Nayer* 42

Little Bear and the Umbrella,
 a fantasy 52

SKILLS: **Vowel Sounds** 62

Word List 64

Kate sees little red things.
Kate calls to me.
Then I see the little red things.
Where do the little red things go?
What are the red things?

Then Kate calls, "Where are you, Ben? What are you doing?"

We call out,
"What are you doing, Ben?"

Ben jumps and jumps.
Now Kate and I are red, too.

Ted likes to paint.

Ted calls, "Who paints your house? Do you paint it?"

The man says, "I don't paint.
Ben paints.
Ben paints my house."

"I paint my big house, but you can paint my little house," calls Nan.

Ted says, "I can paint a little house, but where is it?
I don't see a little house."

"That is my little house," says Nan.

Ted says, "I can paint your little house.
I like birds, and I like to paint."

The man says, "I have a little house you can paint, too. Can you paint two things?"

"I can paint two things. I like dogs, and I like to paint," says Ted.

Ted says, "I don't paint big things,
but I do paint little things.
I can paint one little house or two.
I like dogs and birds,
and I like to paint!"

How to Tell the Top of a Hill

The top of a hill
Is not until
The bottom is below.
And you have to stop
When you reach the top
For there's no more UP to go.

To make it plain
Let me explain:
The one <u>most</u> reason why
You have to stop
When you reach the top—is:
The next step up is sky.

—John Ciardi

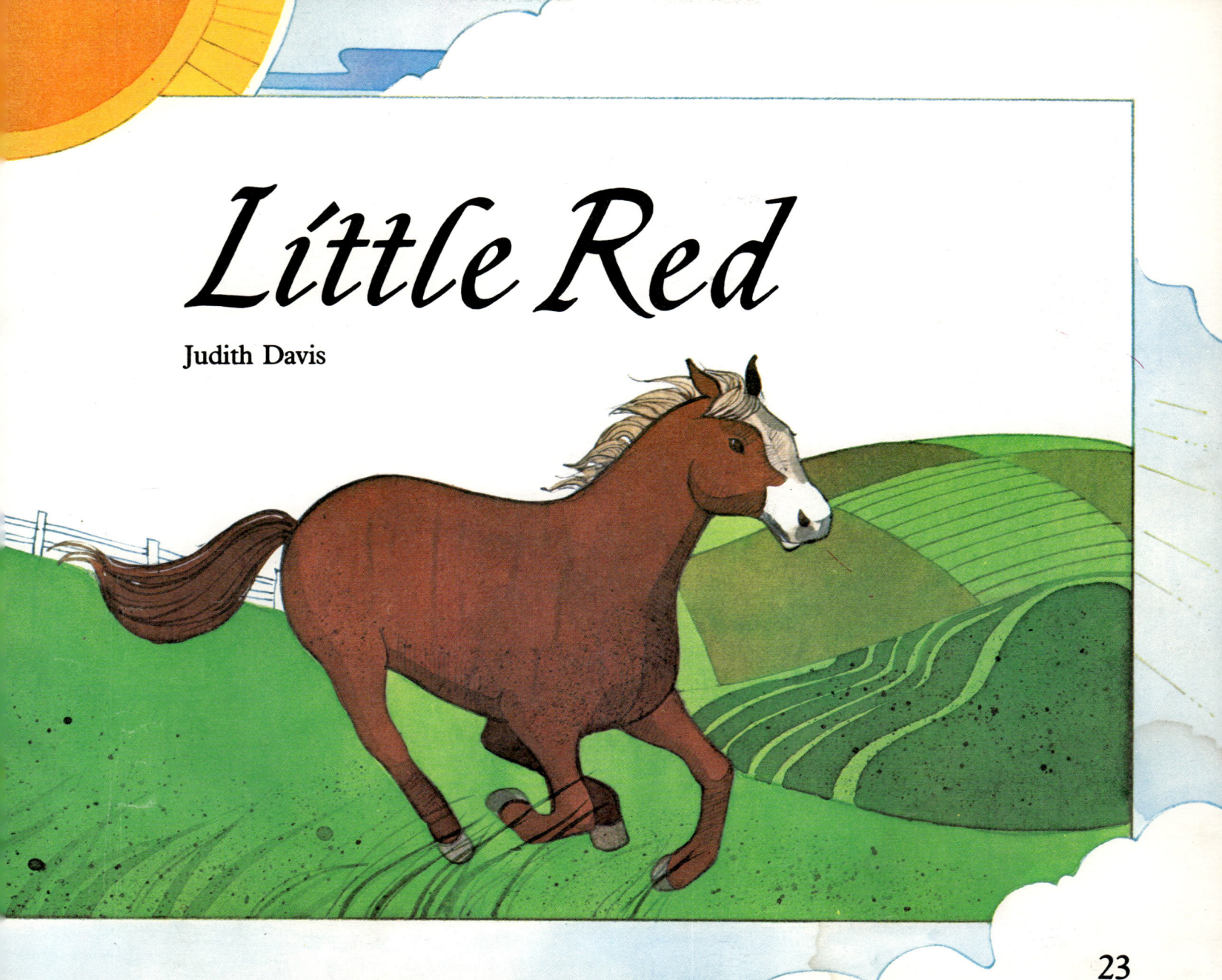

Little Red

Judith Davis

The boy looks at the pony.
"Out!" he calls.
"Don't do that, Little Red!
Go home!
Go home to Kim!"

"Look at that pony," says the man.
"Where does the pony live?"

The boy looks and says,
"It is Little Red.
Did Kim see you run down the hill, Little Red?"

"Little Red is lost," says the man.
"Where does Kim live?"

The boy says, "Kim and the pony live up that hill.
May I ride Little Red?
May I ride Little Red home?"

"You may ride the pony home," the man says.

The boy rides the pony home.
"You are home now, Little Red,"
he says.
"Why did you go out?
Why did you run down the hill?"

"Little Red! Little Red!" calls Kim. "Where did you go?"

Little Red looks at Kim. "What do you have now? You are a funny little pony," says Kim.

Beginning Sounds

Hear	Read	Write
(pan)	<u>p</u>aint walk	<u> paint </u>

   Ted   doing   1. _____

   word   hill   2. _____

   too   read   3. _____

   man   park   4. _____

30

 Read	 Write
[h][k] Ted sits at __ome.	Ted sits at home.

[c][z] 1. Ted can't go to the __oo.

[K][R] 2. He calls __ate.

[p][m] 3. Ted and Kate __aint.

[j][d] 4. Ted paints a __og.

[h][c] 5. Kate paints a __ar.

In the Country

Judith Davis

Bob and Nan can see things in the city.
Bob and Nan will see things
in the country, too.
Bob and Nan like to walk in the country.

Bob walks into the woods.
Nan walks into the woods, too.
Bob and Nan will walk up the hill.
On and on Bob and Nan will walk.

Up on the hill Bob and Nan sit down.
Nan looks out and sees the big woods.
Bob sees the lake,
but he can't see the car.
The car is too little to see.

Bob and Nan can go out on the lake.
Nan likes to fish on the lake.
Birds come to the lake.
The birds come to fish, too.
Bob likes to see the birds.

Nan sees the big house.
Nan likes that country house.

The man calls out,
"Now walk on down
and come on home.
Two and two
will come on home."

Bob looks up.
He likes what he sees.
He likes what he can see
in the country.

City

In the morning the city
Spreads its wings
Making a song
In stone that sings.

In the evening the city
Goes to bed
Hanging lights
About its head.   —Langston Hughes

Judith Nayer

THE PARTY

Kim calls,
"Come with me, Suzy."

43

"Where will we go?" says Suzy.
"Will we go to the lake?
Will we go to the park
or to the zoo?"

"You will see," says Kim.
"Come with me!"

Suzy walks with Kim.
The girls walk on and on.
Then Kim says, "We are at my house.
Come in, Suzy."

Suzy walks in.
In the house Suzy sees three girls.
In the house Suzy sees three boys.
Suzy sees three presents, too!

"A party!" says Suzy.
"Is it my party?"

"It is your party!" says Kim.

"It is a party with presents!"
say the boys and girls.

"Look at the present," say the girls.

"It is a hat!" says Suzy.
"It is a red hat.
I like it!"

48

"Look at that present," say the boys.

"It is a car!" says Suzy.
"It is a little car.
I like it!
Now what is **that**?"

"That is your present, too," says Kim.

"It is a little dog!
It is **your** little dog!
Look, Suzy!
The little dog likes you."

"I like my three presents!"
says Suzy.
"I like my party!
I like **you**!"

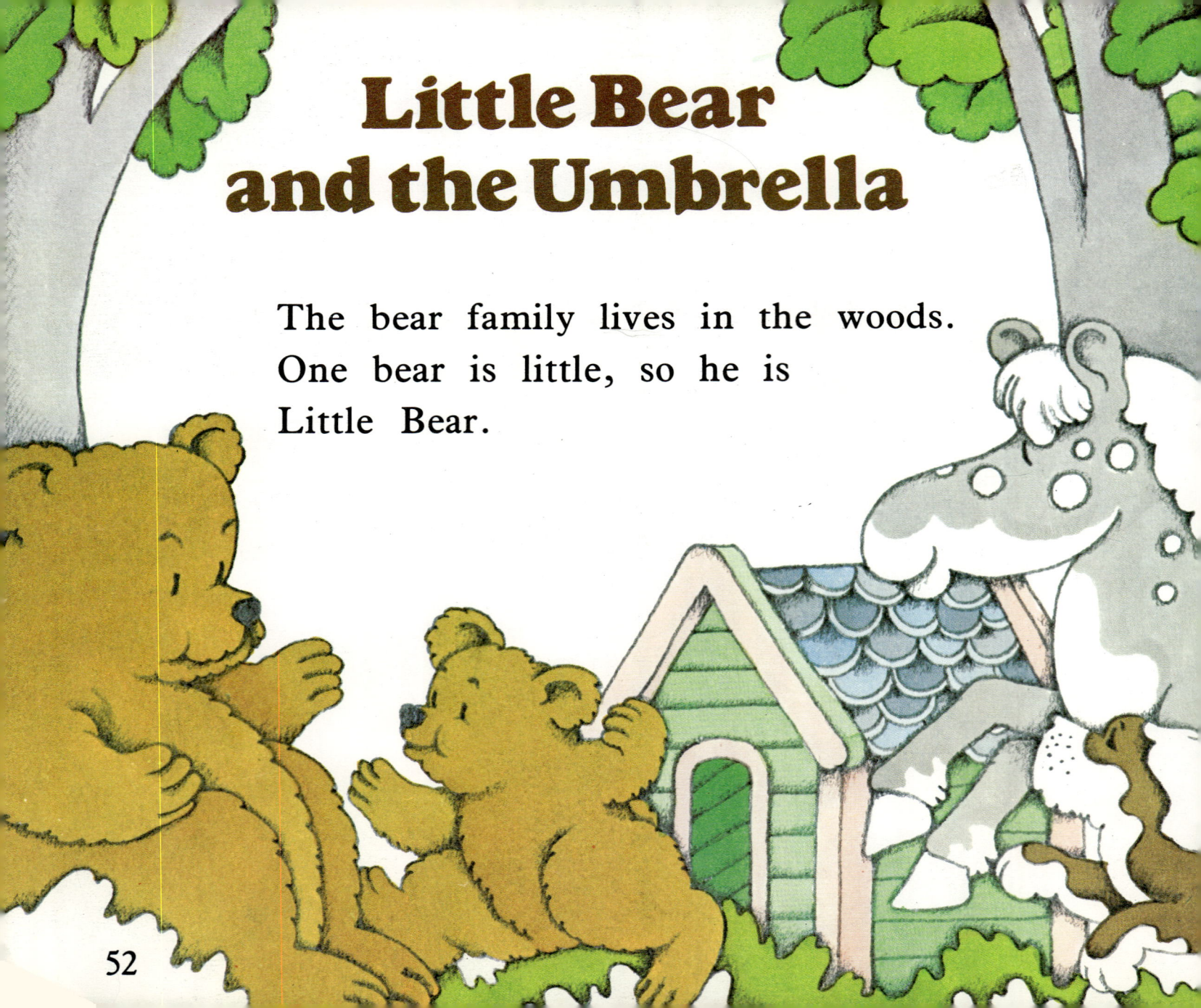

Little Bear and the Umbrella

The bear family lives in the woods. One bear is little, so he is Little Bear.

A pony lives in the woods.
A dog lives in the woods.
A bird lives in the woods, too.

"Look at that," says Little Bear.
"What is it?
Is it a game?"

"That is a funny game,"
says the dog.

"Is it a house?" calls Little Bear.

"That is a funny house," says the pony.

The bird says, "You don't see a house.
You don't see a game.
You see my umbrella."

"I like your umbrella,"
says Little Bear.
"What are the words
on the umbrella?"

The bird says, "You can read,
so read the words."

Little Bear says,
"One, two, three, fly with me."

"Look at Little Bear!
He can fly!" says the dog.

"Up and up I go," says Little Bear.
"What did I do?"

One, two, three, fly with me.

"The umbrella did it," says the bird.
"The umbrella can fly.
You are with the umbrella,
so you can fly, too."

Little Bear calls, "I like to fly,
but can I come down now?
I can't see my house or my family."

"Little Bear, come down
so you can see your family.
Come home!" calls the big bear.

The bird calls,
"You can read, Little Bear.
Read the words and you will
come down."

Little Bear says,
"Three, two, one, down we come."

Little Bear says, "What a ride!
I like to fly, and I like
your umbrella.
But a little bear likes home!"

Three, two, down we come.

Vowel Sounds

Hear	Read	Write
	T<u>e</u>d man	<u>Ted</u>
	did Bob	1. _____
	Bob jump	2. _____
	like Ted	3. _____
	sit dog	4. _____

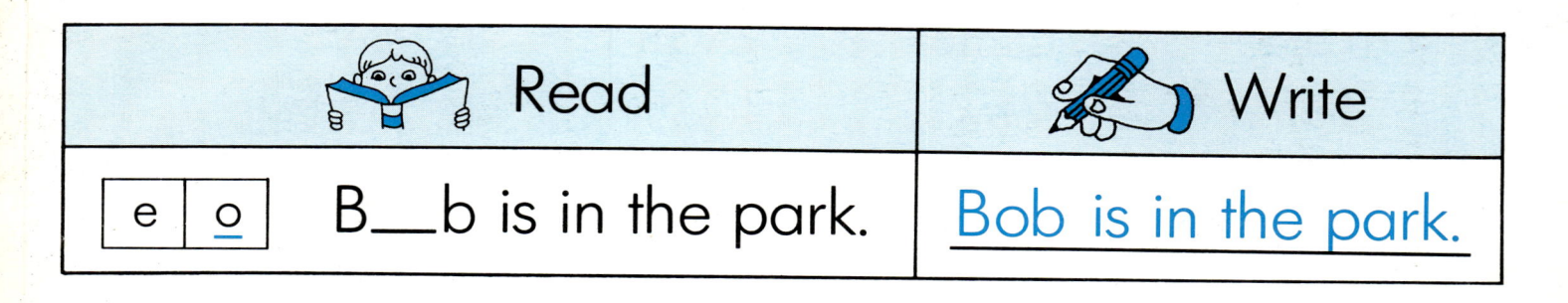

	Read		Write
e | <u>o</u>	B__b is in the park.		<u>Bob is in the park.</u>

o \| e   1. B__n and Ted sit in the park.

i \| o   2. The boys s__t and read.

e \| o   3. Th__n it rains.

i \| o   4. B__b walks up to the boys.

o \| i   5. He sees a b__g umbrella.

WORD LIST

6. me	24. home	will	47. say
then	Kim	35. woods	48. present
7. doing	25. pony	on	52. bear
8. your	26. live	37. come	umbrella
13. paint	did	42. party	family
14. don't	27. may	43. with	so
my	32. country	Suzy	54. game
17. two	34. Bob	46. three	56. fly

To the Teacher: The words listed beside the page numbers above are instructional-vocabulary words introduced in *We Can Read*.

6. red	12. Ted	25. looks	52. lives
8. sits	paints	46. presents	

To the Teacher: The children should be able to independently identify the applied-skills words listed beside the page numbers above by using previously taught phonics skills or by recognizing derived forms of words previously introduced.